The Story of Easter

Christopher Doyle and John Haysom

Introduction

The story of Easter is about the end of Jesus' mortal life on earth. The beginning of this story took place not with His birth at Christmas, but thousands of years before, in the Garden of Eden, when people chose to sin instead of obeying God.

In Old Testament times, God sent prophets to teach people about His plan for the salvation of the world. To fulfill the prophecies, the Father sent His own Son to live as a man so God Himself could to teach His people face=to=face.

Jesus taught people about the kingdom of God, travelling around the towns, villages and countryside. He taught in parables, stories the people could relate to their lives. He showed His power over nature, healed sick people, and even brought the dead back to life. He showed God's love in a way people had never understood before— by dying on a cross to pay for their sins.

Jesus knew He was going to Jerusalem to die. Through His death, He earned God's forgiveness for all of us.

This is the Easter story.

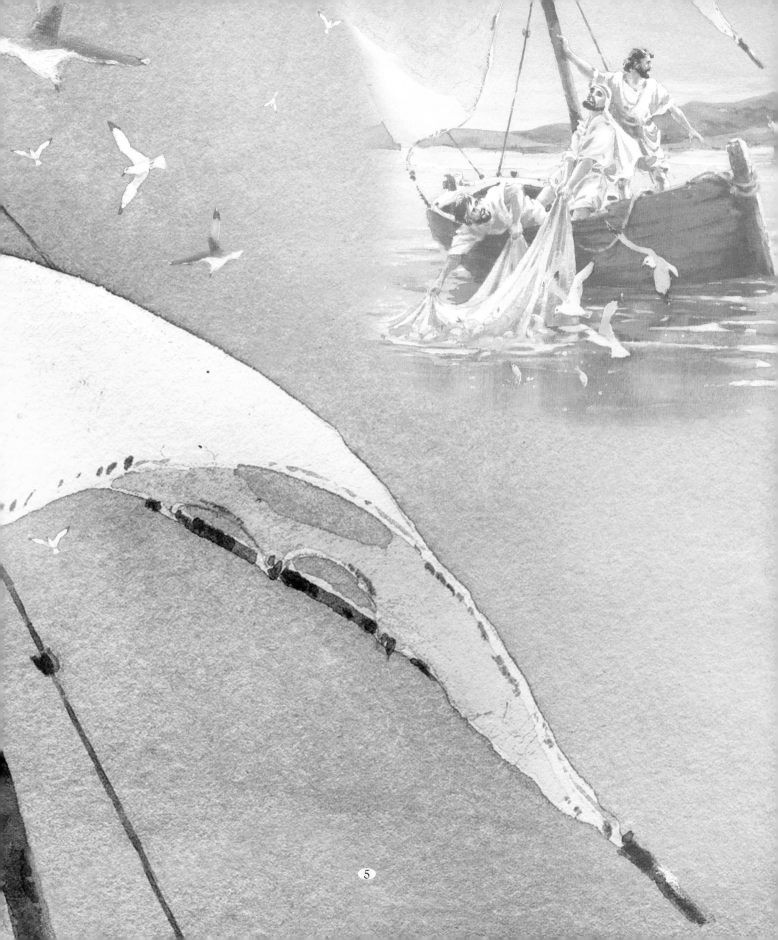

"Can you hear the noise?
He must be close by now!"

The crowds had waited outside Jerusalem
for hours. People nearby had cut branches
from trees. The children waved them
in the air, swatting flies and wafting
a cooling breeze over their faces.
Now, at last, it seemed their waiting
had been worth it.
The cheering grew louder and children craned
their necks to see. In the distance, dust rose under
trampling feet. Shawls and cloaks were laid on the road.
Suddenly they could see their King!
"Look! Jesus is here!" They cheered and
shouted. "Hosanna!"
Sure enough, there was Jesus riding
on a donkey. It was not the way people imagined
their King would arrive but they didn't care.

6

Young and old,
rich and poor, all
turned out to see
Jesus. The large
crowd thronged
around Him.
"Hosanna! Blessed is
He who comes in the name
of the Lord!"

Some people inside the gates of
the city hadn't heard about what
was happening.

"What's all the noise? Who
is causing such a stir?" they asked.

"It's Jesus, the prophet from
Nazareth in Galilee," others shouted
back, and they surged on through the
streets following Jesus toward the temple.

7

In a few days' time it would be Passover.

Many people had come to the temple, as they were taught in the Law of Moses. They needed special temple coins, birds and animals to offer as sacrifices. Traders had set up their stalls; voices echoed through the courtyard and entrance halls. Money-changers counted their coins and clerks scribbled down the accounts for their masters. Amid all this activity came Jesus.

Suddenly there was a mighty crash! Coins, pens and inkpots scattered in all directions. Tables were overturned and cages holding pigeons broke open as they hit the stone floor. All was chaos as birds and animals flew and scampered about.

"The Scriptures say this should be a house of prayer to God," roared Jesus. "You have made it a hiding place for thieves!"

8

The traders were
overcharging and cheating people
of their money. Some of them glared
at Jesus as He
chased them from the temple.
Just then other belivers came
to Jesus. Sick people struggled through
the crowds. Jesus welcomed all of them,
forgave their sins, and healed their illnesses,
making blind people see and lame people walk
again. And children shouted, "Hosanna
to the Son of David."
Watching from the shadows were the
chief priests and teachers of the Law. They
were angry at what they saw Jesus doing.
"We must do something about this
man," they muttered to one another,
"before He causes more trouble. . . ."

During the days that followed, Jesus taught His apostles and the crowds that flocked to see Him about the Kingdom of God. He used parables—stories they easily understood. But His teachings annoyed the temple leaders. Before Passover, they met at the house of Caiaphas, the high priest, to work out a way to stop Jesus. They discussed how they could convince the Romans to arrest Jesus and put Him to death. They knew they must take care how they handled it so as not to cause a riot. But all agreed they should look for the right time and a way to carry out their plans.

Meanwhile, in Bethany, Jesus and His disciples were enjoying a meal at Simon the leper's house. As they ate, a woman came in carrying a jar carved from alabaster. Everyone watched her and wondered what was about to happen. The woman opened the jar and very gently poured oil over Jesus' head. As it trickled down His hair, the scent of the perfumed oil filled the room.

Suddenly the disciples were all talking at once.

"What a waste of expensive ointment!" said one.

"We could have sold that oil and given the money to the poor!"

"Don't be angry with her," said Jesus. "This woman has done a beautiful thing. You will always have the poor here to look after, but soon I shall be gone. She has prepared My body for burial."

One of the apostles, Judas Iscariot, decided then and there to help the Jewish authorities capture Jesus. He went to see the chief priests.

"I can give you Jesus," he said. "How much will you pay me to do it?"

They counted out thirty silver coins and handed them to Judas. From then on he looked for an opportunity to betray Jesus.

11

The next evening, Jesus and the disciples gathered for the Passover, a special meal remembering the time God delivered the Israelites from the death of their eldest child and led them out of Egypt.

A man in the city showed the disciples a room where they could get everything ready and they busied themselves with the preparations. When evening had arrived, and everyone was there, Jesus was sad. He knew God had given Him the power to do all the things He had accomplished and that very soon He would be going back to God.

He also knew the devil had already prompted Judas to betray Him.

Before the meal, Jesus stood up and took off His outer coat. Pouring water into a basin, He started to wash the feet of each of His disciples in turn and drying them with a towel. When it was Peter's turn, he reacted dramatically.

"Lord, I shall never let You wash my feet!"

"You don't understand what I am doing now, but in time you will," replied Jesus. "And if I don't wash your feet, you cannot be My disciple."

"In that case wash them and my hands and head too!" cried Peter.

"I don't have to do that because you're already clean. But not all of you here are clean," He said. That puzzled some of the disciples, but Jesus knew that Judas was guilty.

Jesus sat at the table and explained that as He had washed their feet like a servant would, they should care for others. It was a way to help teach them about the work they would have to do when He had left them. Jesus said, "I tell you the truth, no servant is greater than his master."

Now the food was all laid out on the table. Jesus gave thanks for the meal, and the meal began.

Later, in a quiet moment, Jesus took some of the bread in His hands. He blessed it and then broke it up.

"Take and eat. This is My body, given for you," He said. "Do this to remember Me."

He took a cup of the wine, blessed it, and held it out to them. He explained it was His blood of the New Testament. "This is My blood," He said, "which is poured out for the forgiveness of sins."

Each of the disciples ate and drank. Then Jesus said something that upset and confused them.

"One of you here will betray Me."

They all whispered amongst themselves, wondering whom Jesus meant. Through the chatter, Jesus turned and told Judas to get on with what he was going to do.

Since Judas was in charge of the money, the others thought he was going to buy more food or give some money to the poor. They didn't really pay much attention as he went out.

But that isn't what Judas left to do.

After they ate
and sang a hymn,
Jesus and the disciples
set off through the night to the
Mount of Olives. When they
arrived, Jesus turned to the disciples and
spoke of His death and resurrection.

"Do you realize that all of you will desert Me later tonight?"
He asked. Everyone protested and said they wouldn't. Peter declared
he would never leave Jesus. He seemed very sure of himself.

"You say that now, but before the rooster crows twice in the morning
you will have denied three times that you know Me."

They came to the garden called Gethsemane. Jesus took Peter, James
and John apart from the rest. He admitted to His three friends how
anxious He was. He knew that all of this was God's plan, but it was
still difficult to bear.

"Keep watch here," said Jesus, and He went off a little way by Himself.

In the moonlight Jesus prayed desperately. "Father, I know You can change what is about to happen, but if that is how it has to be done, then I will do it."

Jesus went back to see His friends but now they had fallen asleep. Why couldn't they stay awake for just a while? Jesus prayed again and again, but whenever He returned, the disciples couldn't keep their eyes open.

"Are you still asleep? Come on, the time has arrived. Look, here comes My betrayer."

Over the hill came a band of soldiers carrying spears and swords. Jesus stood and waited. Out of the shadows into the torchlight stepped Judas. He came forward, gave Jesus the kiss of friendship, then slunk away. This was the sign the troops had been waiting for. Now they surged forward to arrest Jesus. He didn't resist — but the disciples all ran away.

The soldiers wasted no time in marching Jesus to the high priest's house.

Although all the disciples had run away, Peter returned and followed the soldiers, keeping out of sight. Now he found himself in the courtyard of that same house. He was grateful for the fire there and he warmed his hands as he sat alongside some of the onlookers.

Just as he was settling down, a servant girl came out of the house. She looked straight at Peter and exclaimed that she had seen him with Jesus.

"Who? Him? I don't know Him," Peter declared, shuffling his feet.

After a little while a man peered at Peter. "You are one of the group that went around with Jesus."

"No, I am not," Peter protested and cursed himself. He was starting to feel uncomfortable but he still sat there, the fire keeping away the night chill.

18

About an hour later, another man finally spoke up.
"You know, I'm certain you were with Jesus.
I can tell by your accent you come from Galilee."
"I don't know what you're talking about!"
Peter was outraged. But as he spoke, from the
distance came the sound of a rooster crowing in
the early morning. Jesus turned, looked out of
the open doors and stared straight into Peter's
eyes. At that moment Peter remembered what
Jesus had said to him earlier in the night.
Peter was devastated. He turned and fled
from the courtyard and broke down in tears.
Meanwhile, as morning grew light, the
chief priests and scribes gathered and led Jesus
off to question Him at their council meeting.

19

The council tried to trick Jesus into saying something they could lay as a charge against Him. They twisted His words and dragged Him away to Pilate, the Roman governor.

Pilate questioned Jesus but could find nothing wrong with His answers. When he discovered Jesus was from Galilee, he tried to pass the problem on to King Herod, the ruler over Galilee, who was in Jerusalem at the time.

Herod had heard about Jesus and wanted to see Him perform a miracle. However, Jesus would do nothing, not even answer the questions Herod asked. The members of the council accused Jesus of all sorts of crimes He hadn't committed. Finally Herod became bored and sent Jesus back to Pilate.

By now the elders had raised a large crowd. They were calling to have a murderer released, as was the custom, and to have Jesus crucified. Because Jesus was not guilty, Pilate suggested a different punishment and ordered that Jesus be whipped.

The soldiers dressed Jesus in a purple robe. One of them braided thorn twigs into a crown and pushed it onto His head. They taunted Jesus, saying, "Hail, King of the Jews." They beat Him and spit on Him. Then Pilate took Jesus out to the crowd.

"Look," said Pilate, "I don't think this man has done any wrong." But the crowd was angry. They told Pilate that if he let Jesus go free, he was not a friend of Caesar. This really worried Pilate because Caesar was the emperor and Pilate answered to him.

"Here is your king!" Pilate said. Seemingly with one voice, the crowd roared back that Jesus should be crucified.

"Shall I crucify your king?" asked Pilate. But he didn't expect an answer. They shouted that Pilate should release Barabbas, who had committed many serious crimes. To please the crowd, he ordered that Jesus be handed over to be crucified.

In the street Jesus staggered under the weight of the cross. He was made to carry it to a hill called "The Skull" outside the city, where He would be crucified. The crowd followed and taunted.

At the hilltop, Jesus' hands and feet were nailed on to the cross. Then He was lifted up and hung between two other prisoners crucified that day. The three crosses stood out starkly against the sky on the top of the hill for all to see.

Pilate had written a sign, "Jesus of Nazareth: King of the Jews," which was fastened to the cross. The rulers of the temple asked why Jesus didn't save Himself as He had saved others. And as the shadows lengthened, the soldiers threw dice and gambled to see which one would have Jesus' clothes.

The women who had followed Jesus out of the city stood watching everything. Jesus' mother was there too. Jesus looked down at her. Then, lifting His head to speak to

His disciple John, He asked him to look after her as his mother.

Then Jesus cried out, "It is finished!"

It was over. Just as the Old Testament prophets had said, God's plan of salvation was carried out through His Son. Jesus, who was God, died for the sins of all that they might be forgiven.

Later, before it grew dark, Joseph of Arimathea took Jesus' body down from the cross. Wrapping it in a linen cloth, he took it to a tomb he had prepared for his own burial. Then, finally they rolled a large stone across the entrance to seal the tomb.

23

Very early in the morning on the third day after Jesus' death, Mary Magdalene crept out of the house. She carried spices and ointments to put on Jesus' body as there had been no time to prepare Him properly for burial. In the dawn light things looked different; all was quiet.

When Mary arrived at the garden, she stopped and gasped. The stone had been rolled away and except for a linen cloth the tomb was empty.

Mary stood outside and wept.

She was startled when two angels asked why she was crying. She sobbed that she didn't know where Jesus had been taken. Then Mary saw that someone was standing behind her. She turned and through her tears looked at a man who spoke to her.

"Why are you crying? Who are you looking for?" He asked.

In her confusion and distress, Mary thought it was the gardener.

"If you have moved Him, tell me where you have put Him," she pleaded. The man spoke again but said only one word.

"Mary!"

Instantly Mary recognized
Jesus and fell to her knees. Jesus had
died and had risen from the dead.

"Teacher," she cried, now tears of
joy running down her cheeks.

Jesus told Mary to go back and tell the others
what she had seen and that He would visit them
again before He went back to His Father in heaven.
Mary ran faster than she ever had before and poured
out the whole story to the apostles. "I have seen the
Lord!" she said. "He is risen!"

The apostles marvelled at Mary's story. Later that evening most of them were together in the upper room of a house. They had the doors locked, scared the Jewish authorities might come after them too. Suddenly, without any warning, Jesus was standing with them in the room.

"Peace be with you," He said. He showed them the wounds the nails had made in His hands and feet and where the Roman soldier had stuck a spear in His side. The disciples were overjoyed to see Him again and talked

26

about the work Jesus had prepared for them to do after He left.

But Thomas had missed the excitement.

"It can't be true," he said. "I won't believe you until I see Him myself."

About a week later, as before, the doors were locked but this time all the disciples were together. Again Jesus came in, stood there with them and said, "Peace be with you!"

"So, Thomas, you doubt your friends. Here, put your fingers in the marks on My hand. Touch this scar on My side."

"I don't need to; I can see it is You, my Lord and my God."

Jesus told Thomas, "You believe because you see Me. Plenty of others will believe without seeing Me, and they will be blessed because of it."

Then Jesus left them again.

D ays passed and the disciples went back to their work as fishermen in a village by the Sea of Galilee. One evening they set off in the boat and worked hard all night, casting their nets but catching nothing. As the day dawned, they were at the point of packing everything up when a man called from the shore.

"Try casting your net on the other side of the boat."

The disciples were worn out but they did as the man said and cast the net once more. When they hauled it in this time, they couldn't believe it; the net was so full of fish it nearly broke!

John shielded his eyes against the sun. "Hey, Peter!" he cried. "Look, it's Jesus!"

Without another thought, Peter jumped into the water and waded ashore, leaving the others to haul the catch to the beach.

Jesus invited them to have breakfast. He already had fish cooking over a small fire and some bread too.

As they talked, Jesus asked Peter, "Do you love Me?" Peter said he did. Two more times Jesus asked this and Peter said, "Yes, Lord. You know I love You." Jesus told Peter to take care of His followers and said, "Follow Me."

Some days later, Jesus returned to be with His Father in heaven. He told the disciples to return to Jerusalem and wait for the Holy Spirit to come. He would bring them power and help in the work they had to do.

When the Holy Spirit arrived on Pentecost, the disciples couldn't contain themselves. They went out and told the good news about Jesus to everyone and baptized them in the name of the Father, the Son, and the Holy Spirit. That is the story of God the Son who came to bring forgiveness of sin to the world. That is the story of Easter.